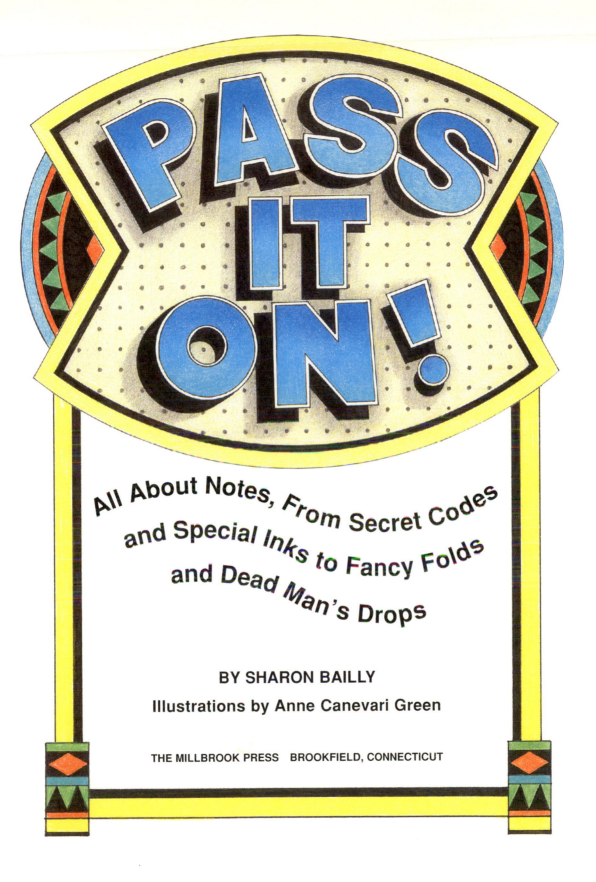

PASS IT ON!

All About Notes, From Secret Codes and Special Inks to Fancy Folds and Dead Man's Drops

BY SHARON BAILLY

Illustrations by Anne Canevari Green

THE MILLBROOK PRESS   BROOKFIELD, CONNECTICUT

To Ophelia Bailly (thank you for the note)
and to Gene Trupin (thank you for the book)

Library of Congress Cataloging-in-Publication Data
Bailly, Sharon.
Pass it on! : all about notes, from secret codes and special inks
to fancy folds and dead man's drops/by Sharon Bailly :
illustrations by Anne Canevari Green.
p.   cm.
Includes bibliographical references and index.
Summary: Examines the history of writing and provides instructions
for making special inks, using various alphabets and codes, and
creating personal seals and private letter drops.
ISBN 1-56294-588-2 (lib. bdg.)
1. Cryptography--Juvenile literature. 2. Writing--Juvenile literature.
[1. Cryptography. 2. Writing.] I. Green, Anne Canevari, ill. II. Title.
Z103.3.B35   1995 652'.8--dc20   94-46949   CIP   AC

Contents

1

A Note
to You

The next morning a note, most fearfully and wonderfully twisted and folded...[was] passed across to Anne.... Anne read the note...and dispatched a prompt reply back to the other side of the school.
L. M. Montgomery, *Anne of Green Gables*

Notes are written on notebook paper, folded neatly, and passed from friend to friend at school. Notes are written in code and smuggled from spy to spy. Notes are inked on handmade paper and carried on a silver tray by a servant. Notes are clipped to the refrigerator, saying: "Spaghetti for supper; don't be late, OOXXX, Mom."

Notes are fun. Everybody writes them and likes getting them. Other people go crazy wondering what's inside them. A note seems to call out, "Peek at me! Peek at me!"

You don't need big reasons to write a note, just a piece of paper, a pencil, and a thought to share. Sometimes the note is this simple: "Hi! What's up? I'm bored. Write back soon."

Sometimes the note is so secret that you wish you had a secret code to write it in. This book shows you actual spy codes. It tells you how to make your own paper for the notes you send; find invisible ink in your kitchen; set up your own mailbox in your backyard; and uncover the hidden meanings in your handwriting. What if your *y*'s have long bottom loops? What if your handwriting runs uphill? What if you leave the dot off your *i*'s? How did the *i* get its dot anyway?

And why is a note called a note?

The English word "note" comes from a Latin word (*nota*) that means "mark." Long before people wrote notes on paper, they wrote messages by marking or notching lines on a stick. All over the world—Europe, Asia, Africa, Australia—people passed notched sticks, just the way we pass notes on paper today.

So in a way, when you write a note, you are acting out the very beginnings of world history. Now there's an excuse to try on your teacher!

2

Making Paper

"And I was so sorry, that I took and wrote on a piece of sycamore bark, 'We ain't dead—we are only off being pirates,' and put it on the table by the candle."

Mark Twain, *The Adventures of Tom Sawyer*

This book you are holding is made of paper. The notes you pass are written on paper. Paper comes mostly from trees. You really have to mash a tree hard to make paper.

When people first started writing, they put their marks on things that were easy to find:

- Leaves
- Flattened stems of plants like papyrus and bamboo
- Stones
- Bones
- Clay tablets
- Walls

Leaves and stems tore easily. Stones and bones were hard to mark. Clay tablets and walls were heavy to carry around, especially walls.

Honest, They Really Did

If you want to see the different ways people wrote long ago, you can. You'll have to travel, though.

If you want to see how:	You should visit:
People wrote on walls	Pyramids in Egypt
People wrote on stone	Rosetta stone, displayed at the British Museum in London, England, or the Egyptian obelisk (Cleopatra's Needle) in Central Park in New York City
People pounded bark into paper	An ancient mortar, displayed at the Imperial Museum in Honan, China
People first wrote on paper	Paper made in A.D. 262 in China, now in the Royal Library, Stockholm, Sweden; a Swedish explorer dug it up

So people tried writing on things that were stronger, easier to mark, and lighter:

- Thin sheets of bronze

- Sheepskins and goatskins (called parchment)

- Cloth, such as silk

Bronze had to be pounded flat; skins had to be washed, stripped of hair, scraped, stretched, and rubbed soft; and cloth had to be woven from thread. With all that work, bronze, skins, and cloth cost more than stones or clay. Besides, how long would you want to keep an old sheepskin around, even if your best friend in the whole world wrote on it?

Ts'ai Lun Makes Paper From a Mulberry Tree

About A.D. 100, a man in China named Ts'ai Lun gathered bark from a mulberry tree and stems from the hemp plant. He soaked the bark and the hemp in water and beat them into small pulpy pieces. He lifted the pulp out of the water on a screen, and dried it in a frame to shape it. After the pulp dried, Ts'ai Lun peeled off a light, thin sheet—the first paper.

Making one sheet of paper took Ts'ai Lun a long time. But bark and hemp cost less than bronze or silk, and they were easier to prepare than skins. The paper lasted longer than leaves or stems and weighed less than stones.

Now we make paper from chips of pine, poplar, spruce, oak, and many other trees. The chips of wood are soaked in water and chemicals until they separate into threadlike pieces, called fibers. The fibers are pressed together and dried to squeeze out the water they soaked up—about 4 1/2 pounds of water for every pound of paper (almost 4.5 kilograms of water for every kilogram of paper). It takes a lot of water and wood to make a sheet of paper.

But if you would like to make paper almost the same way Ts'ai Lun did, you can.

How You Can Make Paper

To make one or two sheets of writing paper you will need

A pan or basin with a wide opening (for example, a turkey roasting pan) that will hold a gallon (about 3.75 liters) of water

A piece of screen (just small enough to fit in your pan)

1 gallon of lukewarm water

4 sheets of tissue paper (the kind found inside gift boxes)

Liquid laundry starch or cornstarch (if you use liquid laundry starch, you might want to wear rubber gloves)

An electric mixer or eggbeater

Three pieces of cardboard (about the size of your screen)

Here's what you do. Read the steps carefully first to find out the hard parts.

1. Cut the piece of screen so that it is small enough to slip easily in and out of the pan.

2. Pour the gallon of water into the pan.

3. Tear the four sheets of tissue paper into many pieces and put the pieces in the water.

4. Beat the water and paper for at least 2 minutes with the electric mixer or eggbeater. The tissue paper should turn pulpy.

5. Add 2 tablespoons of laundry starch or 3 tablespoons of cornstarch to the water and paper. (The laundry starch produces a nicer paper, but may be harder to find.)

6. Beat the water and paper another half minute.

7. Put a piece of cardboard down near the sink, where water can run off it without making a mess. In a little while, you'll need the cardboard to help dry off your writing paper.

8. At an angle, slip the wire screen under the water. (If you drop the screen into the water flat, the pulp will be underneath it; you want the pulp on top.) Move the screen gently from side to side so that the paper floating in the water covers the screen.

9. Lift the screen straight up and set it down on the cardboard.

10. Put another piece of cardboard on top and press hard. Use a rolling pin if you have one. Water will squish out.

11. This is the first hard part: Lift the top piece of cardboard off the wet paper. The cardboard will stick, so you will have to peel it gently. Once you remove the wet piece of cardboard from the top, repeat Step 10 if you want.

12. Peel the piece of paper off the screen, then lay it back on the screen and let it dry. Allow four hours at least. (That's the second hard part—waiting.)

13. Pick up your piece of paper. Write on it!

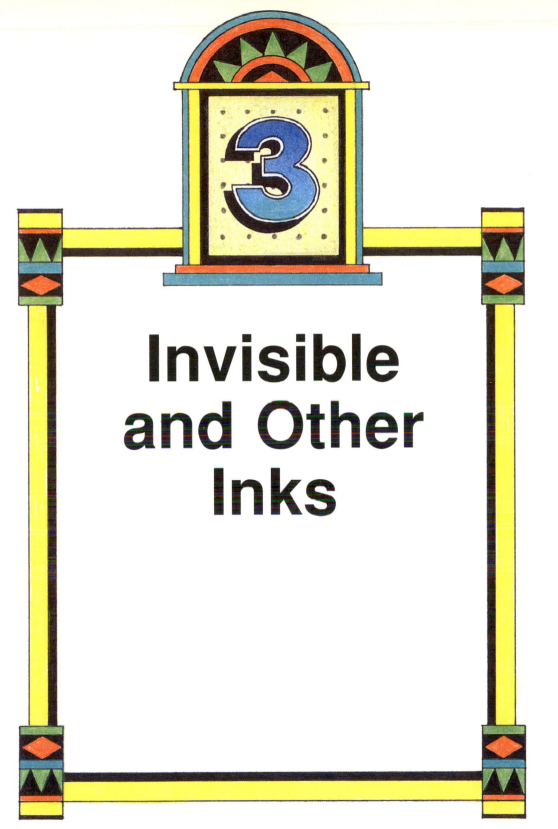

Invisible
and Other
Inks

Paddington tried writing his name with the invisible ink and he couldn't see it at all.

Michael Bond, *More About Paddington*

As Paddington the Bear discovers, invisible ink has good points and bad points. With invisible ink, the words you write disappear; your note is safe from snoops. But it helps to know how to make the words reappear when you want to read them. If you want ink that disappears and reappears, just take a stroll out to the kitchen.

Lemons and Lightbulbs

One plump lemon will give you lots of invisible ink.

1. Squeeze the juice of a lemon onto a plate.

2. Dip a toothpick (or small brush) into the juice.

3. Write on paper with the toothpick. You won't be able to see what you're writing unless you look hard. If the lemon juice is too watery to write with, stir in a little sugar to thicken it.

When the lemon juice dries, no one will be able to see the words you wrote. Heating the paper makes the words reappear. Hold the paper so that it touches a hot lightbulb. (Keep your fingers at the ends of the paper, away from the bulb. You don't want to burn your fingers.)

Milk is an especially good invisible ink. As you did with the lemon juice, write your note by dipping a toothpick or brush in the milk. Let the note dry. When you want to read the note, take the shavings from a pencil sharpener. Sprinkle the shavings over the paper, then throw them away. Where the shavings of pencil lead touched the milk, the letters you wrote will show up light gray.

16

An everyday pencil, just 7¼ inches (18.4 centimeters) long, can write 45,000 words.

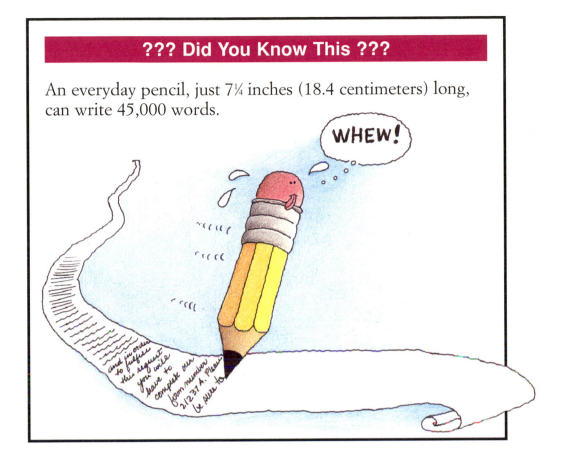

Invisible ink won't last forever. Old ink may not react to a light-bulb or pencil shavings. Don't wait too long to send your note!

Greeks, Persians, and Lollipop Wrappers

Invisible ink lets you hide your message. The paper you write on looks completely blank. But there are other ways to hide your message. You can write it in code. The paper clearly has words on it, but no one can tell what the words mean unless they know your code. Chapter 7 describes lots of codes. Or you can write your message and cover it with a fake message. No one who sees your note will think to search for two messages.

About 450 B.C., the Greeks were fighting the Persians. A former king of the Greeks, named Demaratus, worked for the Persian army. (He didn't like being a former king.) One day, he learned that the Persians planned a major attack on the Greeks. For some reason, he decided to warn the Greeks. Maybe he felt bad about working for the Persians, or maybe he wanted to brag about how much he knew.

In any case, Demaratus cut his warning into a wooden tablet. He knew that if he sent the tablet, the Persians would read the warning and stop it from reaching the Greeks. So he covered the tablet with wax, and wrote a second message in the wax. As the tablet was carried from hand to hand, only the harmless words in the wax could be seen.

When the Greek general received the message in wax, it puzzled him. But the general's wife figured out what Demaratus had done. She scraped off the fake message in wax and found the warning carved into the wood.

Here's a way for you to hide your messages. You will need a piece of paper, a pencil, a red crayon, a red marker or felt-tipped pen, and a piece of cellophane. You can get the cellophane by cutting out the see-through window from a window envelope. Or save the see-through wrapper from a lollipop.

1. Write your message on the paper lightly in pencil:

2. Cover the message by scribbling over it with the red crayon. Try to turn your scribble into a picture, so anyone looking at the note will think you are passing a picture.

3. Now color the cellophane red with the marker.

4. Lay the cellophane on top of the picture. Your pencil message will show through.

No cellophane anywhere? You can still hide a message with a message. You'll need (a) a pencil and (b) a pen that writes in washable ink. Write your real note lightly in pencil. Then use the washable ink to cover the note with words or drawings. To uncover the real note, hold the paper under the water tap until the washable ink washes off.

By the way, if you write your note in red pencil on green paper, or in green pencil on red paper, 8 percent of the boys (about one boy in twelve) won't be able to read it, even if they find it. Those boys are color-blind.

A Few Points About Pencils

The first lead pencils really were lumps of lead. These pencils were wrapped in paper to keep fingers clean. But lead pencils don't have any lead in them now. They contain graphite sandwiched between two pieces of wood.

Graphite, a mineral, was discovered under the ground in England in the 1500s. That was the only graphite mine known in the world for many years. In fact, graphite was so rare that the English miners were searched at the end of every workday to make sure they didn't steal any. It was so in demand that people even sold fake pencils—pieces of wood with a little graphite smeared on the end.

In the 1790s, in France, Nicholas-Jacques Conté mixed graphite with clay and baked it. The pencils made with this mixture wrote as well as the old pencils, but they used less graphite.

Today, graphite comes from mines in Mexico, China, Siberia, and Madagascar. Graphite isn't rare anymore, but it has some very rich cousins—diamonds! Both graphite and diamonds are made up of pure carbon.

TAP TAP TAP

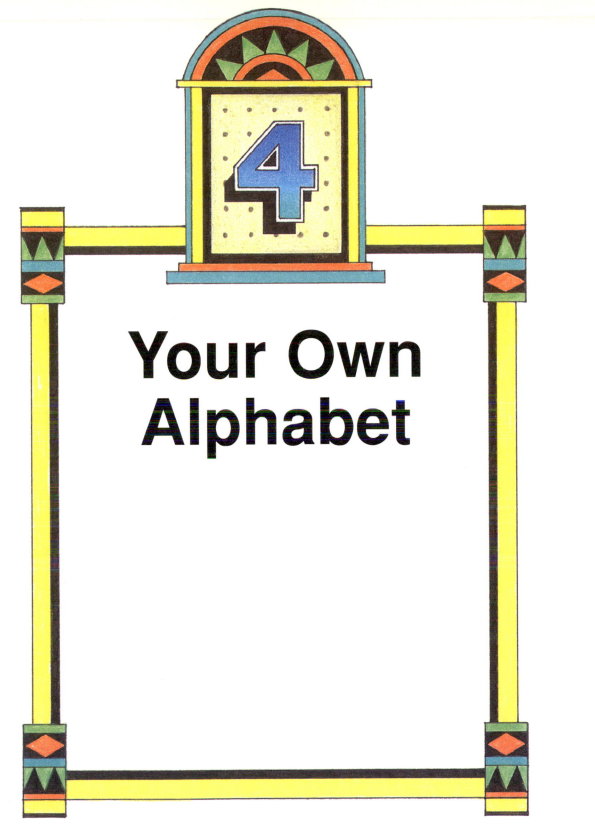

4

Your Own Alphabet

[Rabbit] saw a piece of paper on the ground. And there was a pin in it, as if it had fallen off the door....This is what it said:

> *GON OUT*
> *BACKSON*
> *BISY*
> *BACKSON.*
> *C.R.*

A. A. Milne, The House at Pooh Corner

C.R. (Christopher Robin) wrote that note to his friend Rabbit before he learned how to spell. He wanted to write, "Gone out, back soon, busy, back soon." But he forgot the *e* in "gone"; he put "back soon" together as one word and left out one *o*; and he spelled "busy" with an *i* instead of a *u*.

Still, some things about his note look just fine. All the letters are from the ABCs. All the words start at the left side of the page and move to the right. If you wrote Christopher Robin's note, you might spell better; but you, too, would start writing at the left side of the paper.

Why is English written from left to right? The Chinese write their words from the top of the page to the bottom. The Arabs write from right to left.

The idea of an alphabet began in the Middle East where words were written from left to right. Phoenician traders showed this alphabet to the Greeks. The Greeks tried several ways of writing: left to right, right to left, and boustrophedon (boo-stro-fed-on).

How to Write Like an Ox

That last word means "ox-turn." The Greeks wrote the way a farmer plows a field: He steers the ox straight down one row, turns the ox around to the next row, and sends him back the way he came. The Greeks wrote their first line of words right to left; then they turned every letter around and wrote the next line left to right, and so on.

How English Would Look

Written Up and Down

Y a t s
o   n   h   e
u   o   e   e
    t   n
c   e   c   C
a   o   h
n   t   d   a
    h   e   p
w   i   i   t
r   s   t   e
i   ;   r
t   w
e   a   3.
    y

Written Right to Left

Hold this to a mirror.

Written Boustrophedon

Sometimes we go this way,
and sometimes that.

The History of A and B

The first letter of the alphabet may have begun as a drawing of an ox. You can see the ox's horns in the first drawing.

GREEK   ROMAN   MEDIEVAL   MODERN

The people who used this sign called it 'aleph—their word for ox. The letter ' is not in the alphabet any longer. Over time, aleph changed to look like the letter *A* we use today. The name of the letter also changed from aleph to alpha to *a*.

The second letter of the alphabet may have begun as a drawing of a house, and was called beth—the word for house. Maybe you can see the pointy roof of the house in the first drawing below.

GREEK   ROMAN   MEDIEVAL   MODERN

Again, beth changed until it looked like the letter *B* we use. Its name changed to beta and then to *b*.

By putting the words alpha and beta together, we get the word alphabet.

By and by, the Greeks decided to write left to right all the time (it was easier than boustrophedon). They taught their version of the alphabet to the Romans; and the Roman armies brought it to England. And that is the reason we all write English left to right. However, if you wanted to write a secret message to a friend, you might try the other ways.

24

Or if you wanted to write a really secret message, you could make up a brand-new alphabet. That's how we got the ABC's in the first place: People made them up.

The Alphabet Gets Some *Z*'s and Dots Its *I*'s

As the alphabet traveled from country to country (from the Phoenicians to the Greeks and Romans, and then to the English), it gained and lost letters.

Latin, which the Romans spoke, sounded different from Greek. The Romans didn't need the sound of the sixth letter of the Greek alphabet, which was written as Z. First, the Romans threw the Z out. Then they changed their minds and took it back to use when writing words borrowed from Greek. They tagged it onto the end of the alphabet. That's why our alphabet goes from *A* to *Z*.

The letter *i* arrived in the alphabet in two pieces. It started as a straight line. It earned its dot in the 1400s to keep it from looking like *n* or *u* when it hooked up with other handwriten letters. If you write the word *skiing* in script without the dots, you can see just what the problem is.

25

Every letter in the alphabet has some history, but you can make history of your own. You can make up your own alphabet.

The more people you tell about your alphabet, the more people will be able to read it. If they like it a lot, they may start to use it and tell their friends about it. Then maybe three thousand years from today, your alphabet will be in a book along with the ABC's.

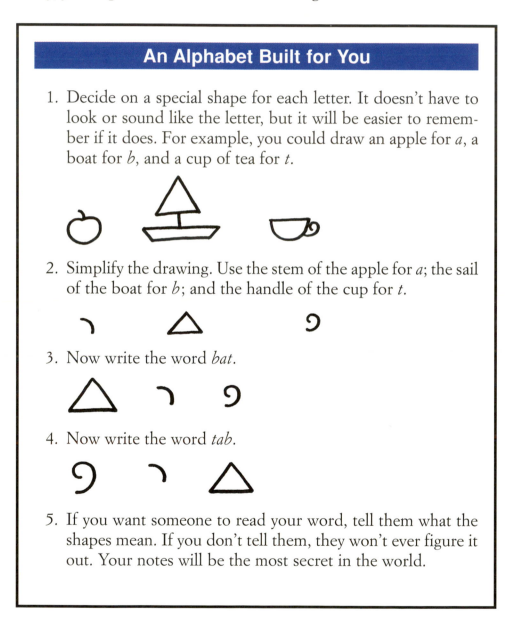

An Alphabet Built for You

1. Decide on a special shape for each letter. It doesn't have to look or sound like the letter, but it will be easier to remember if it does. For example, you could draw an apple for *a*, a boat for *b*, and a cup of tea for *t*.

2. Simplify the drawing. Use the stem of the apple for *a*; the sail of the boat for *b*; and the handle of the cup for *t*.

3. Now write the word *bat*.

4. Now write the word *tab*.

5. If you want someone to read your word, tell them what the shapes mean. If you don't tell them, they won't ever figure it out. Your notes will be the most secret in the world.

5

What Your Handwriting Means

This note, prettily written on scented paper, was a great contrast to the next, which was scribbled on a big sheet of thin foreign paper, ornamented with blots and all manner of flourishes and curly-tailed letters.

Louisa May Alcott, *Little Women*

Do you write your notes with curly-tailed letters? Do you cross your *t*'s with a long strong line but forget to dot your *i*'s? Do you write the REALLY IMPORTANT stuff in all capitals?

Whether it's neat or sloppy, large or small, your handwriting tells secrets about you. Graphologists are people who study handwriting. Graphologists believe that the way you shape your letters tells what you are like. Letters with big curly tails (*y*), for example, show that you have strong feelings. Graphologists may be right or wrong about what they find in handwriting, but one thing is sure—it's fun to look.

Do you want to uncover a few handwriting secrets? First, look at your own handwriting. Then you'll know what to look for in the handwriting of friends. You'll need a sample of your handwriting, so write on a piece of paper:

The quick gray fox jumps over the lazy brown dog.

That sentence has every letter of the alphabet.

Everything About *U*

What can you learn from a single letter? Take the letter *u*. Different people will shape it differently. Open loops, some graphologists say, are a sign of an open person. If you put loops in your *u* (*u*), you are open and friendly and feel close to people. If your *u* is neat and even (*u*), you are neat and orderly in your thoughts. If the sides of the *u* squeeze together (*u*), you keep your lips closed and your thoughts to yourself.

Like the letter *u*, the letter *t* is a tattletale. The cross bar of the *t* can be long or short, heavy or light, straight or crooked. If your

28

cross bar is short and sticks close to the rest of the letter (*t*), it may show that you are a careful person, shy and timid. If the cross bar is long and firm (*t*), you may be firm in your decisions. If you forget the bar, you are often rushed and careless. Some graphologists say that a bar that's wavy, like a silly smile (*t*), shows a good sense of humor; and a bar that's thicker on one end, like an angry slash (*t*), hints at a quick temper. If your *t* looks like a capital *A* (*A*), standing sharply on two legs, you may be stubborn.

Don't Forget to Dot Your *i*'s
(and Mind Your *p*'s and *q*'s)!

Here's what some graphologists believe the little dot over the *i* can tell about you.

Does this look like

Your *i*?	Your dot?	It means this:
i	To the left	You are cautious; you put off doing things.
i	To the right	You are curious; you look ahead.
i	A line	You are tense and worried.
i	A circle	You are artistic and like to be different.
i	A curve	A dot like a smile? You have a good sense of humor.
i	An arrowhead	You have a sharp tongue and are easily annoyed.
i	No dot	You are lazy or careless.

29

Letter by letter, your handwriting scatters clues about how you think and feel. But some clues can be found only in groups of letters and whole pages of writing.

Big Loops, Big Thoughts

Look at the lowercase *h*, *d*, *b*, *f*, *k*, *l*, and *t* in your handwriting. These letters have lines or loops that reach up. When the tops of your letters soar up high, so do your thoughts and dreams:

The quick gray fox jumps over

The force that drives your letters up also drives your mind toward new ideas. People who write tall letters like to study, but they often like to study alone. They might grow up to work in a laboratory, program computers, write books, or paint.

How the *S* Changed from a *Z* to a Snake

When you first started writing, you copied the shapes of letters. Using those shapes, you came up with your own handwriting. But what makes those shapes the right ones? How come an *s*, for example, is shaped like a snake? Why not shape it like a swordfish or a sausage?

In fact, around 1000 B.C., the *s* was shaped like a *w* and pronounced *shin*, the Phoenician word for tooth. Then it gradually moved to its side. Kids who learned to write in those days wrote the *s* with angles, as if it were a backward *z* (⊆). That was the best *s* shape they could make because they wrote by pressing a stick into a clay tablet. A pointed stick pressed into hard clay makes letters with sharp angles: ▷ ℞

When brushes and paper replaced sticks and clay, the new writing tools let people form rounder letters. The *s* took on its present snake-like shape (S). Then pens came along. With pens, people could draw skinnier, finer letters than they could with a brush. Try writing the same sentence with a pen, a pencil, and a crayon. Your handwriting will appear different every time.

Now you have a way to change your handwriting if you want to. Just change the tools you write with. You could also

- Practice a fancier handwriting

- Change from writing separate letters to writing letters linked to each other (change from printing to cursive)

Write Like a King

One reason your handwriting looks the way it does today is because of a powerful king and an abbey full of monks. From about A.D. 771, Charlemagne (Charles the Great) reigned as king of the Franks. He wanted brand-new, beautiful books for his castle.

He asked the monks in the abbey of St. Martin at Tours in France to make the books. Because there weren't any machines for printing books in those days, the monks copied each book by hand. They had pens, so they could write nice round letters. But some monks wrote more neatly than others.

The monks thought: "If we all make our letters the same way, the books will look much prettier." Together, they practiced a very neat handwriting until each monk wrote beautifully. They named their new handwriting Carolingian in honor of Charles the Great (*Carolus* is Latin for *Charles*).

If you find a new handwriting you like and practice it, you can change your handwriting, too.

Make Sure All the Letters Hold Hands

Back when people wrote with sticks, they would write one letter, lift the stick, then write the next letter, and so on. If you try to write your name in the soft ground with a stick, you will feel the stick catching against the soil. You have to stop after each letter to pull it out. But people became so used to writing one letter at a time that they continued to write that way even after they switched from sticks to brushes and pens.

In the 1400s, the clerks of Italy broke this habit. The clerks earned their wages by writing for other people. Instead of writing words one letter at a time, they linked the letters together. As a result, they wrote faster and more neatly, and they earned more money. Soon everyone linked the letters—what we now call cursive writing. Changing from printing to cursive will make your handwriting look different, too.

Folding
a Note

"Here's a note to you, Meg, all sealed up."
Louisa May Alcott, *Little Women*

If ever the best things come in small packages, notes do. You fold a note to hide the message and to make the note easier to pass from hand to hand.

You can fold your note over and over into a scrunched-up ball. Or you can fold it into a special shape that carries good wishes with it.

The Chinese were probably the first to fold paper into special shapes, but the Japanese developed paper folding into an art form. The Japanese have been folding paper for at least nine hundred years. Their word for paper folding is *origami*.

Japanese children enjoy origami. The shape they like to fold the most is the crane (*tsuru*), a water bird with a long graceful neck. The crane brings good luck. The Japanese believe that if you want a wish to come true, you should fold and string together a thousand cranes (*sembazuru*). Japanese children leave *sembazuru* at the Peace Park in Hiroshima, Japan, to wish for peace. At the end of this chapter are the steps for folding a lucky crane.

In Japan, paper folding also plays a part in the religion of Buddhism. Priests fold flowers to place around statues of Buddha in the temples. They cut out paper figures of the gods. They even wear paper robes. The paper must be made from the fibers of special plants, usually the mulberry tree, without the rags and chemicals that go into other types of paper. The paper is *washi*—a name that means "handmade."

Usually, origami begins with a square piece of paper, but the paper can be other shapes, even round. Most often the paper is colored on just one side. When the paper is colored on two sides, each side is really a very thin sheet of one color pressed to a second thin sheet of another color.

The first fold in origami is the most important. It is either a diagonal (corner to corner) or a book fold (through the center). The final shape you want always determines what your first fold should be.

You can fold notes in many ways. Here are folds that look like an ice-cream cone and a pretzel bag. They both start with rectangular paper; they both start with the book fold. As you follow the directions, press down on each fold to make a sharp crease.

After you try these folds for sending your notes to friends, you can fold a box to keep the notes that your friends send to you.

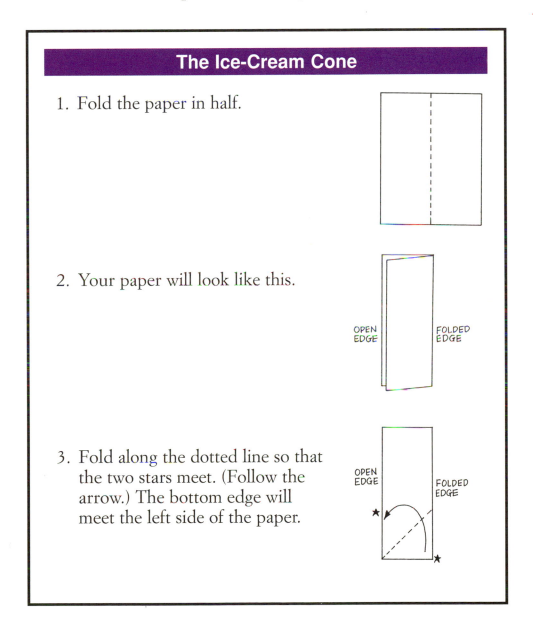

The Ice-Cream Cone

1. Fold the paper in half.

2. Your paper will look like this.

OPEN EDGE   FOLDED EDGE

3. Fold along the dotted line so that the two stars meet. (Follow the arrow.) The bottom edge will meet the left side of the paper.

OPEN EDGE   FOLDED EDGE

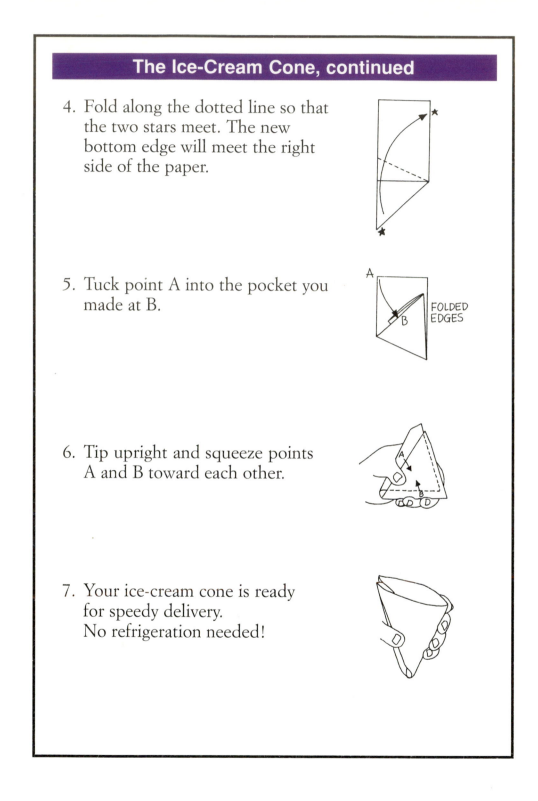

4. Fold along the dotted line so that the two stars meet. The new bottom edge will meet the right side of the paper.

5. Tuck point A into the pocket you made at B.

6. Tip upright and squeeze points A and B toward each other.

7. Your ice-cream cone is ready for speedy delivery. No refrigeration needed!

The Pretzel Bag

1. Fold the paper in half.

2. Now open up the paper again. Fold so that the right edge of the paper meets the crease in the middle.

3. Fold the right side over again.

4. One more time!

5. Your paper will look like this. Press all the folds flat.

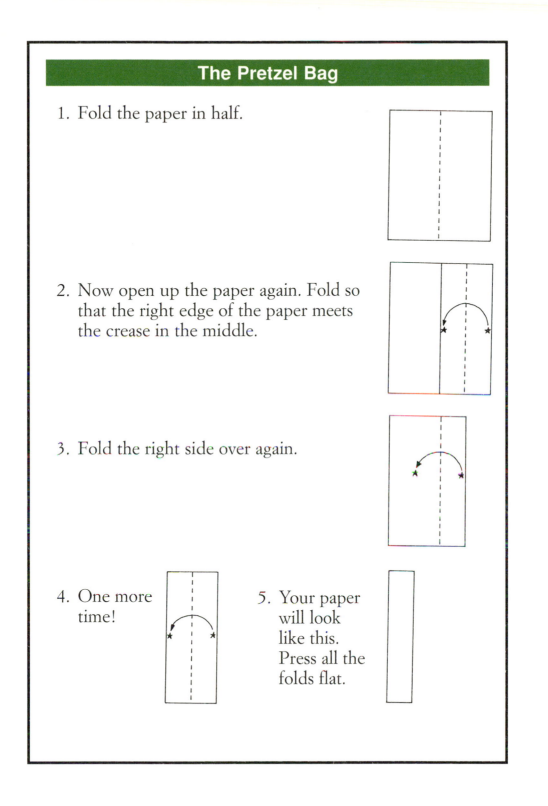

37

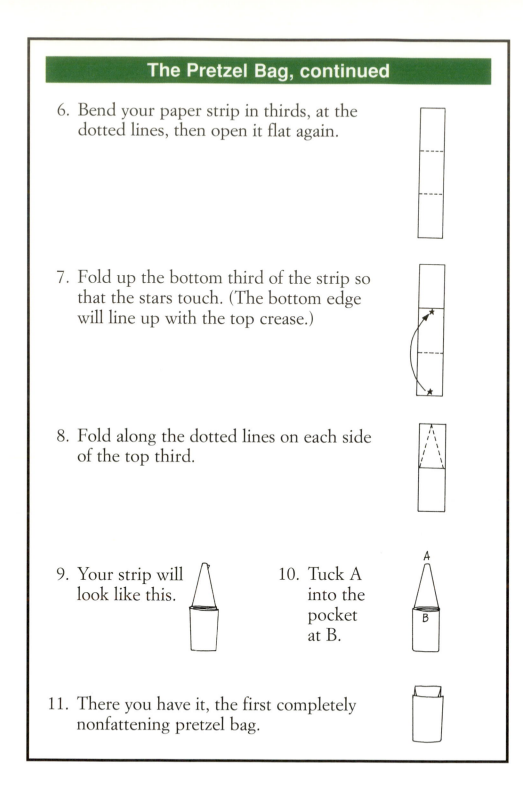

6. Bend your paper strip in thirds, at the dotted lines, then open it flat again.

7. Fold up the bottom third of the strip so that the stars touch. (The bottom edge will line up with the top crease.)

8. Fold along the dotted lines on each side of the top third.

9. Your strip will look like this.

10. Tuck A into the pocket at B.

11. There you have it, the first completely nonfattening pretzel bag.

The Box

You need two pieces of paper that are the same size.

1. First, you'll make the bottom of the box. Fold up each side of the paper, about 1 inch (2.5 centimeters) from the edge. Then open again. The folds on your page will look like this:

2. Cut at the dotted lines.

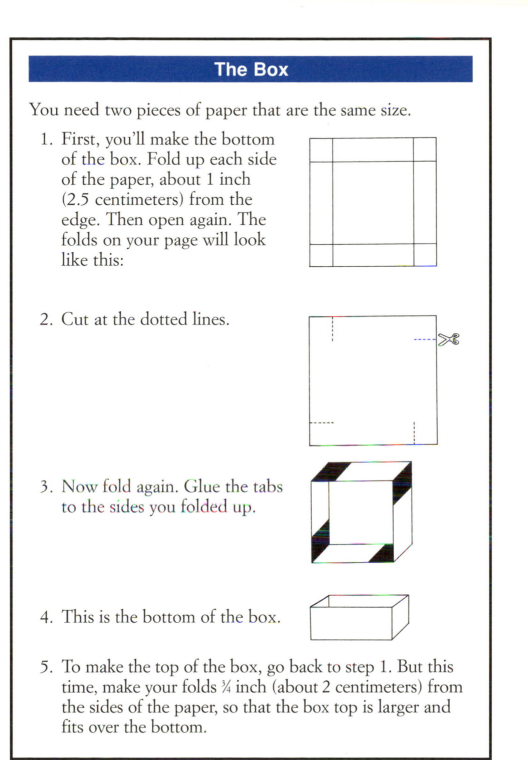

3. Now fold again. Glue the tabs to the sides you folded up.

4. This is the bottom of the box.

5. To make the top of the box, go back to step 1. But this time, make your folds ¾ inch (about 2 centimeters) from the sides of the paper, so that the box top is larger and fits over the bottom.

The Lucky Crane

The crane can be folded many ways; this way is one of the easiest. You'll need a piece of rectangular paper. Notebook paper or typewriter paper is fine, but a sheet 5 inches by 7 inches (13 by 18 centimeters) works well.

Before   **After**

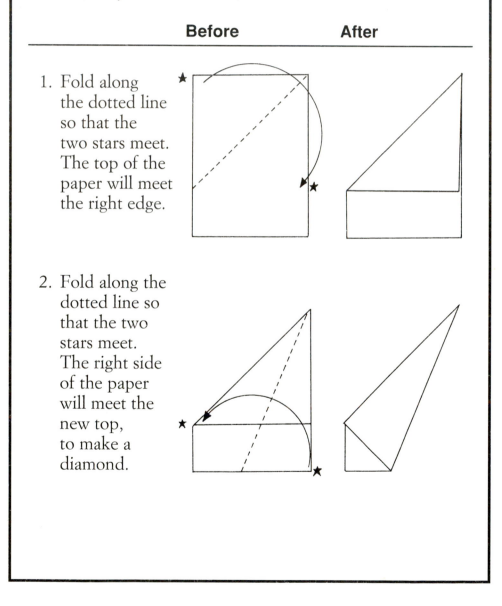

1. Fold along the dotted line so that the two stars meet. The top of the paper will meet the right edge.

2. Fold along the dotted line so that the two stars meet. The right side of the paper will meet the new top, to make a diamond.

3. Turn the diamond so that the long side is next to you. Fold up the narrow end of the diamond along the dotted line.

4. Fold the tip down along the dotted line.

5. Your crane should look like this:

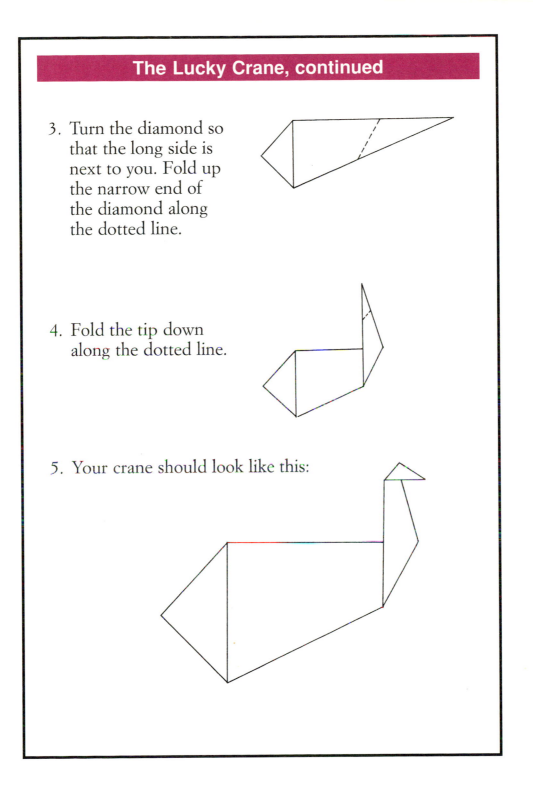

Secret Codes

"If you use the code which I have explained," said Holmes,
"you will find that it simply means 'Come here at once.'"
A. Conan Doyle, *The Return of Sherlock Holmes*

You write a note to a friend, you fold it up, you send it hand to hand, and the wrong person opens it: the class tattletale or even the teacher. If you wrote something you wanted to keep secret, the secret is out!

If you want to protect your notes, you can write them in code. Then, no matter who opens your note, only a friend who knows the code will be able to read it. Codes are so good at hiding messages that, at one time, only kings and queens were allowed to use them. Anyone else who wrote in code risked having his (or her) head cut off.

??? Did You Know ???

When is a code not a code? When it's a cipher.

A code puts one whole word in place of another. A cipher changes or moves one letter at a time. Most often, people use the word *code* to mean both true codes and ciphers. All the codes in this chapter are really ciphers.

You might find true codes handy, also. Does your kid brother tag along when you meet your friends for ice cream? If you and your friends decide that *beets* is your code word for *ice cream*, you might be able to outwit your brother. When a friend asks, "Do you want to go for beets?" you can bet your little brother will stay home.

A Code for Spaced-Out Notes

See if you can read this coded message:

HEL LOB ETH WHA TSU PHA VEY OUS EEN MYP ETC OWX

Believe it or not, the message is written in English. It looks odd because TSU PHA VEY aren't words. This message is written in space code. Spaces are supposed to come at the ends of words; in a space code, they don't. In this example, the spaces are placed after every three letters. The X at the end of the message is to make sure that the last group also has three letters.

If you pretend the spaces aren't there, words begin to appear and the message clears up:

HELLO BETH WHATS UP HAVE YOU SEEN MY PET COW X

Commas, periods, and other punctuation marks are never coded. Codes are easier to break when periods show where one sentence ends and another begins.

Try putting this message into space code:

CAN'T HELP WITH COWS, BUT THERE'S
GOOD GNUS IN THE PAPER.

(Answer [1] at the end of this chapter gives the coded message.)

A Code That Skips to the Right

About two thousand years ago, the Roman ruler Julius Caesar made up a secret code that spies still use. In the Caesar code, each letter of the alphabet is switched with a letter three places on. In English, the Caesar code works like this:

a b c d e f g h i j k l m n o p q r s t u v w x y z

code: d e f g h i j k l m n o p q r s t u v w x y z a b c

To write a secret message, use the bottom code letters in place of the top letters. Try putting this message in Caesar's code:

IF THE COW COMES BACK, SHOULD I DUCK?

The coded message should look like this:

LI WKH FRZ FRPHV EDFN VKRXOG L GXFN

If you want to make a Caesar code even harder to read, add a space code:

LIW KHF RZF RPH VED FNV KRX OGL GXF NXX

A Code That Has Your Number

When each letter of the alphabet is changed to another letter, the code is called a substitution code—one letter just substitutes for another. The Caesar code is one type of substitution code. Another type of substitution code is based on numbers:

a b c d e f g h i j k l m n o p q r s t

code: 1 2 3 4 5 6 7 8 9 10 11 12 13 14 15 16 17 18 19 20

u v w x y z

code: 21 22 23 24 25 26

Now here's a coded message:

15-14-12-25 9-6 25-15-21-18-5 3-8-9-3-11-5-14

Can you figure out what it says? (Answer [2] is at the end of this chapter.)

You can make up your own code with slight changes to these substitution codes. For example, instead of counting three letters over in the Caesar code, count two letters over:

a b c d e f g h i j k l m n o p q r s t u v w x y z

code: c d e f g h i j k l m n o p q r s t u v w x y z a b

Or number the alphabet backwards (*a* would be 26 and *z* would be 1). Just be sure you and your friends are using the same code, or your messages will be so secret you'll never figure them out.

46

A Code That Turns Itself Backwards

Before you code your message, you can switch the words or letters around to make the code even harder for someone to figure out. Try writing your message backwards:

SDNEIRF DEREHTAEF ENIF RUOY OT DNIK EB

This is called a transposition code—a code that moves the letters around. Now put the backward message into a substitution code, like the number code where *a* is 1 and *z* is 26. (Answer [3] at the end of the chapter shows what your code should look like.)

Even if the wrong person breaks your number code, the message still won't make sense, because it is written backwards.

You don't want anyone to figure out your code just by snooping around, so change your code often. You can tell your friends what code you are using each time by changing the color of the pencil or pen you write with. A coded note written in red might mean "This is the Caesar code." A coded note written in blue might mean "This is the space code."

A Code That Turns Cartwheels

Back in the 1400s, Leon Alberti was a writer, an artist, an architect, an athlete, and a musician in Florence, Italy. He also liked to make up and solve new codes. In fact, he is called the Father of Western Cryptology. The word *cryptology* comes from two Greek words: *crypto* means "secret," and *logo* means "word." So Leon Alberti is the "father of secret words."

Alberti invented a wheel for forming new codes. He cut out two circles, one big and one small. He wrote the numbers 1 to 26 around the outside of the big circle. He placed the little circle on top and pinned the two circles together (a paper holder will do the trick if you want to try it yourself). Then he wrote the letters of the alphabet on the little dial, one letter under each number.

Whenever Alberti needed a letter of the alphabet to write a note, he chose the number above it on the big dial. He changed his

The Mr. E Code

When spies want to decode a note, they are helped by knowing that English uses some letters more than others. The most common letter in English words is *e*. It is also the letter that comes most often at the end of a word.

If one letter or number shows up most often in a code, it probably stands for the letter *e*. Can you guess what the other most-used letters are? There are seven more. (See answer [4] at the end of this chapter.)

Spies also know that the most common two-letter words in English are *of*, *to*, and *in*. The most common three-letter words are *the* and *and*. The most common four-letter word is *that*. What are the most common one-letter words? (See answer [4] at the end of this chapter.)

48

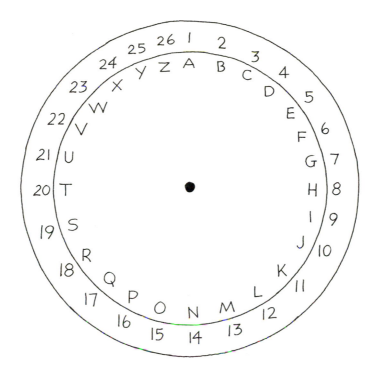

This is an example of Alberti's wheel.

code by moving the dial. Then the same numbers stood for completely different letters.

If you and your friend have the same dials set the same way, you can code and decode secret messages. Every day, both of you should move the dial along one space in the same direction. Your code will change every day. No one will be able to figure it out unless they have a dial set the same way, too.

Switch Codes Now!

But what if someone does break your code? If that happens, you have to warn your friend to change codes fast. You can write a warning word in your note. Choose a word to use only in case of danger. If this word—the control sign—shows up in a note, it means "Switch codes now!"

Short and Secret Codes for Your Notes

ASAP	As soon as possible
BFF	Best friends forever
DSTT	Don't show this to . . . (follow up with the initials of the person who should never, ever, see the note)
FFE	Friends forever
FFFFTOYFF	Fall fatally flat five times on your fat face
fv	On the back of the page (comes from the Latin words folio verso)
I♥U	I love you
IOU	I owe you
N.B.	Note well (comes from the Latin words *nota bene*)
N.G.	No good
PDQ	Pretty darn quick
Q.T.	Quiet
SNAFU	Situation normal, all fouled up
SWAK	Sealed with a kiss
TGIF	Thank goodness it's Friday
T/T/Y/L	Talk to you later
UNMEQT	You (U) and (N) me (ME), cutey (QT)
WBN	Write back now
WBS	Write back soon

All the Answers

[1] CAN THE LPW ITH COW SBU TTH ERE SGO ODG NUS INT HEP APE RXX

[2] ONLY IF YOU'RE CHICKEN!

[3] 19-4-14-5-9-18-6 4-5-18-5-8-20-1-5-6 5-14-9-6 18-21-15-25

15-20 4-14-9-11 5-2

[4] The letters that crop up most often in English words are E,T, A,O,N,R,I,S, in that order. You can remember these letters with the phrase *a sin to er*. How common are they? If you count off one hundred letters anywhere in this book, the letter *e* should occur about thirteen times. The most common one-letter words are *I* and *a*.

8

Dead Man's Drops and Chinese Seals

"If you had dusted the mantlepiece, you would have found this just under the clock," said Gandalf, handing Bilbo a note.

J. R. R. Tolkien, *The Hobbit*

Sending a note is as easy as handing it over, or as tricky as hiding it. Long ago a Persian king sent a note to his general by shaving a man's head and tattooing the note onto the man's bald scalp. The hair grew back and covered the note. Then the man carried the message to the general, without anyone guessing what he hid. To read the note, the general shaved the man's head.

The Persians also carried messages by hand. A man on foot could carry a note more than 30 miles (about 50 kilometers) a day. If a message had to travel a long way,

---

Have You Ever Sent a Message by Arrow-Mail?

The Persians thought up many ways to send notes. One general sent messages to his spy by shooting arrows. He would wrap a note around an arrow and shoot the arrow to an agreed place, where the spy could pick it up. But one day, the general's arrow hit a man instead of the ground. When a crowd ran to help the man, they found the note, and the spy was soon caught.

a new runner was placed every 30 miles (50 kilometers) or so to take over carrying the message.

In China, where people used the same hand-to-hand system, the runners wore bells on their belts. From a long way off, the jingling bells warned the new runner to get ready for a mail delivery. If a message had to go quickly, the sender stuck a feather on it. The feather meant "Carry this letter as fast as a bird flies." Even though the note never left the ground, you could say it went airmail express.

The Spy Who Combed Her Hair

Even when mail could travel by boat and train, spies found hand-to-hand delivery safer. In the 1860s, during the American Civil War, Rose Greenhow spied for the Southern states. One day, she found out that the Northern (Union) army was ready to march South. She asked a young friend, Betty Duvall, to carry a warning to the Southern (Confederate) army. She wrote the message in cipher, folded it into a tiny packet, and sewed it with silk. Then Betty wound her long hair into a bun and placed the packet in her hair, holding it in place with a comb. Dressed as a farm girl, Betty safely carried the message in her hair.

When Rose Greenhow feared that she might be caught, she smuggled all her spy papers out of her house. Some she hid in the folds of her dress, some she asked a friend to carry out in her shoes, and others were carried out in a guitar case.

After she was caught (by Allan Pinkerton, who founded the U.S. Secret Service), Rose Greenhow still sent and received spy messages. She coded them by sewing them into cloth. The colors of the thread gave news of the war. The soldiers guarding her never stopped the traffic in secret messages—after all, it was nothing but sewing!

However—just in case you don't want to shave your head, can't run 30 miles (50 kilometers) a day, and don't sew—there are other ways to deliver a note.

A Secret Mailbox

You could set up your own secret mailbox. Spies call a box for leaving notes a letter box or dead man's drop. You can "mail" a note by leaving it under a rock, in a hole in a tree, or in a gap in a fence. You can slip the note under the doormat at your friend's house. You can hide the note between the pages of a magazine that you leave on a park bench. As long as your friend knows where to look, the place you leave your note is your dead man's drop.

If you want to hand a note to your friend without anyone else knowing, you could let a pen serve as your dead man's drop. Take the ink cartridge out of a ballpoint pen. Roll your note tight and slip it into the pen in place of the cartridge. Now, instead of handing your friend a note, you'll hand over a pen, with the note hidden inside. No one else will know the real reason you are lending your friend a pen.

Is It Really You?

If you are passing notes through a dead man's drop, you want to make sure your friends know the message came from you. You can mark your note with your own special seal that no one else can copy.

A seal is a design stamped on a note or letter. Seals have been used since ancient times. As early as the fifth century B.C., the Chinese made seals by cutting stamps out of brass, stone, or wood. They pressed the stamps on red, purple, or black ink. They used the seals instead of signing their names.

About A.D. 600, the Japanese learned about seals from the Chinese. Seals are still so important in Japan that the people who make them must join a Sealmakers' Union. It takes ten years to become a Master Sealmaker. In Europe during the Middle Ages, people sealed their notes by dripping colored beeswax on the paper. They pressed the beeswax onto the paper with a stamp that might be made of gold or ivory or lead. On the base of the stamp, a picture was carved; this showed up in the beeswax.

At one time, everyone who sent messages owned a personal seal. Some people had one seal for everyday letters and another for secret messages.

Arrows, Pigeons—Bottles! Let's Try Bottles!

In the 1940s, the U.S. Navy put a note in a bottle and threw it in the Pacific Ocean to find out how fast it would travel. The note was written in eight languages, so that anyone who found it would be sure to know who sent it. The bottle bobbed across 1,250 miles (2,010 kilometers) of ocean in 53 days. It landed in the New Hebrides Islands (Vanuatu). The man who found it could not read any of the languages it was written in.

Stamp Your Own Seal

An easy way to make a seal is to find a small stone with a flat side. Press the flat side of the stone on a stamp pad, then on a piece of paper. Each time you press down with the stone, it will leave its outline on the paper.

In addition to stones, buttons and coins (especially foreign coins) leave interesting designs when they are inked and pressed on a piece of paper.

You can make another type of seal by writing your initials on a piece of paper with glue; then sprinkling salt on the paper. When the glue dries, dust off the extra salt. Place your writing paper on top. Scribble lightly with a colored pencil. The pattern of the salt will come through the top sheet and serve as your seal.

A third way to make a seal is by cutting out the same shape several times from colored paper. On the cutout, draw a picture you like that will remind your friends of you. Do you own a cat? Pick flowers? Read books? Ride a bicycle? Draw a picture of one or two of these things on your seal.

Glue or tape the seal to the bottom of the note instead of signing it. Your friends will know who sent the note, but no one else will.

Any of these seals can also be placed on the outside of your note. Fold your note first and then place your seal over the opening. If the seal is broken when your friend receives the note, beware! Someone found and read your note—someone who was not supposed to.

Change Your Name

If you want to sign your note but still hide your name, you could turn your name into an anagram.

An anagram mixes up the letters in one set of words to make a new set of words. Count up the letters in your first and last names. Tear a small piece of paper for each letter. (If your name is

Pat Jones, you need eight pieces of paper.) Write one letter on each piece of paper. Move the pieces around to make words. If you mix the letters in PAT JONES, you get JOT PANES or O SNAP JET.

Now, let's see. You could print your note on the paper you made in the alphabet you thought up, turn it into code, write it in invisible ink, sign it with an anagram, fold it into a pretzel bag, seal it, and leave it for your friend at a dead man's drop behind the wastebasket in math class.

Just let someone try to steal that note!

Books and More Books

Your library and bookstore offer lots of books about paper, ink, handwriting, codes, and the adventures notes can get you into.

Chapter 2

Bourgeois, Paulette. *The Amazing Paper Book.* New York: Addison-Wesley Publishing Co. Inc., 1989.

Chisholm, Jane and Anne Millard. *Early Civilization.* London: Usborne Publishing Co., 1991.

Grummer, Arnold E. *Paper by Kids.* New York: Macmillan Children's Book Group, 1990.

Grummer, Arnold E. *Tin Can Papermaking: Recycle for Earth & Art.* Appleton, Wis.: Greg Markim, Publishers, 1992.

Chapter 3

Carey, Steven. *Kids' America.* New York: Workman Publishing, 1978.

Cobb, Vicki. *The Secret Life of School Supplies.* New York: J. B. Lippincott, 1981.

Chapter 4

Kaye, Carolyn Berger. *Word Works.* Boston: Little, Brown and Company, 1985.

Scott, Joseph, and Lenore Scott. *Egyptian Hieroglyphs.* New York: HarperCollins Children's Books, 1990.

Chapter 5

Burgess, Anna. *The Do-It-Yourself Lettering Book.* Mahwah, N.J.: Watermill Press, 1993.
Morgan, Chris. *Handwriting Analysis.* London: Quintet Publishing, 1992.

Chapter 6

Enomoto, Nobuyoshi. *Origami Playtime.* Rutland, Vt.: Charles E. Tuttle, 1990.
Milord, Susan. *Adventures in Art.* Charlotte, Vt.: Willaman Publishing, 1990.

Chapter 7

Grant, E. A. *The Kid's Book of Secret Codes, Signals & Ciphers.* Philadelphia: Running Press, 1989.
Wrixon, Fred B. *Codes & Ciphers: An A to Z of Covert Communication From the Clay Tablet to the Microdot.* New York: Prentice Hall General Reference & Travel, 1992.

Chapter 8

Bakeless, John. *Spies of the Confederacy.* New York: J. B. Lippincott Company, 1970.
Chang, Ira. *A Separate Battle: Women and the Civil War.* New York: Lodestar Books, 1991.
We Deliver . . . The Story of the U.S. Postal Service. Washington: Smithsonian Institution Press, n.d.

You'll also enjoy these stories:

Blume, Judy. *Blubber.* New York: Macmillan Children's Book Group, 1982.
Cleary, Beverly. *Ramona the Brave.* New York: Morrow Junior Books, 1975.
Herodotus. *History.* Buffalo, N.Y.: Prometheus Books, 1992.
Hope, Anthony. *The Prisoner of Zenda.* New York: Puffin Books, 1984.
Keene, Carolyn. *The Strange Message in the Parchment.* New York: Grosset & Dunlap, 1974 (1993 printing).
Kipling, Rudyard. *Kim.* New York: Dell Publishing Co., 1992.

Index